shapes

a book by John J. Reiss

Bradbury Press Inc. • Scarsdale, New York

To Jimmy Dinsch, Adam Spangler and Maria Esther Herrera

squares

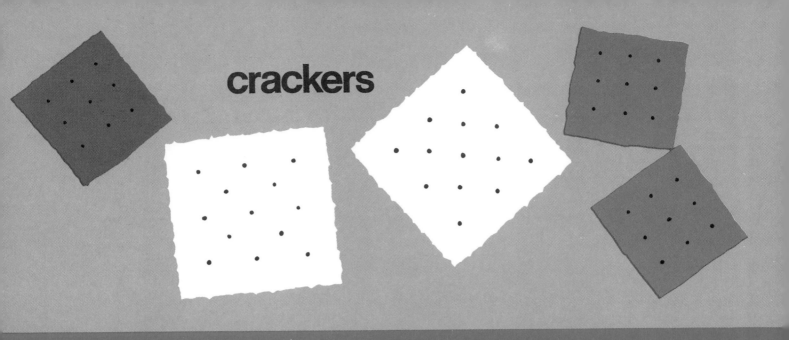

crackers

checkerboard

signal flags

window

squares make cubes

triangles

sails

arrowheads

mountain tops

tents

triangles make pyramids

circles

buttons

spinning wheel

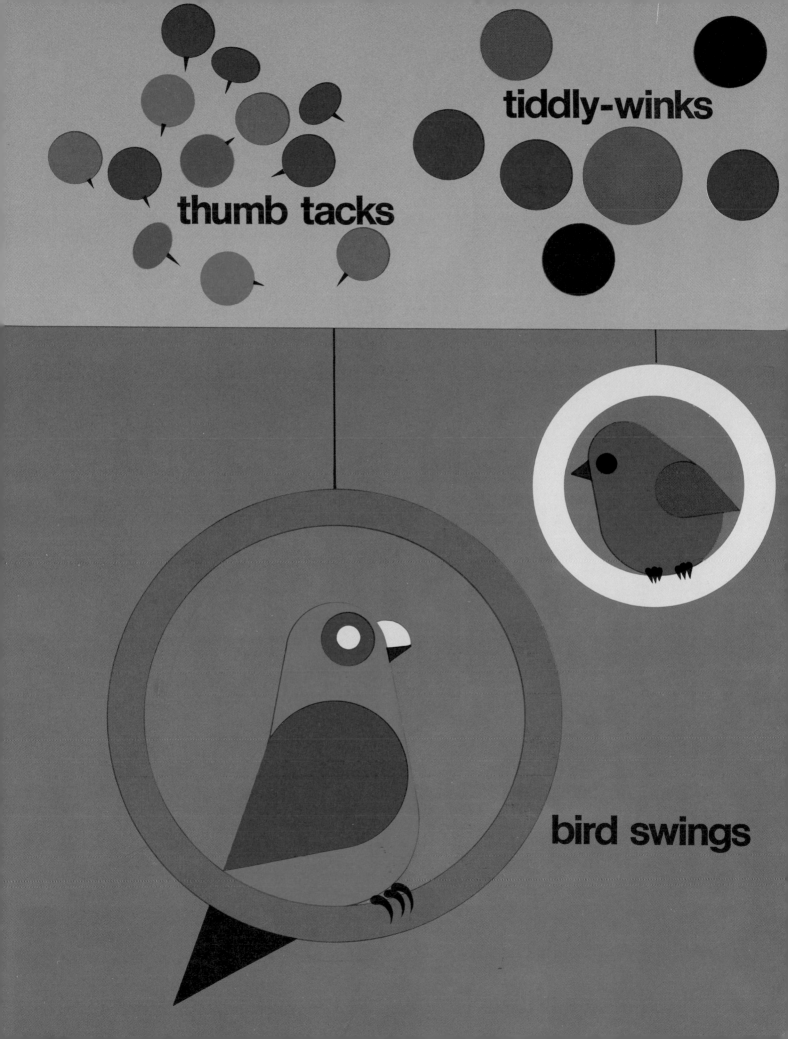

circles make spheres

rectangles

sticks of gum

doors

 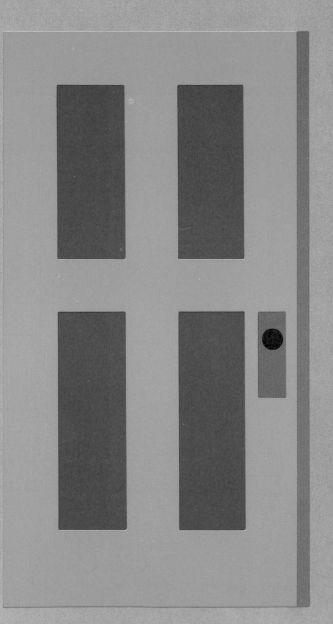

bricks

wooden planks

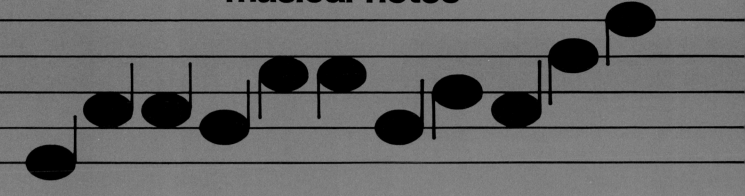

musical notes

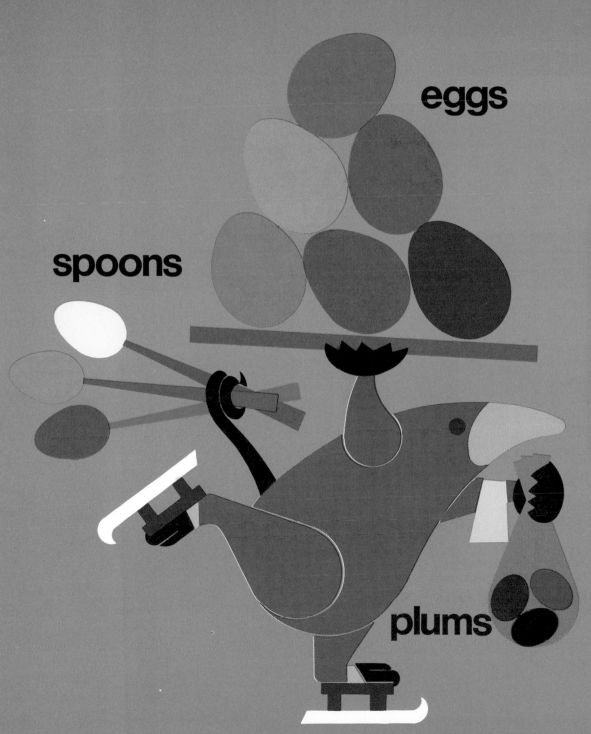

eggs

spoons

plums

more shapes

pentagons

hexagons

octagons

shapes all around